Princes
&
Tides

Princes & Tides

Dawn Taggblom

Poetic Justice Books
Port St. Lucie, Florida

©2018 Dawn Taggblom

book design and layout: SpiNDec, Port Saint Lucie, FL
cover image: *Princess of Tides*, ©2018 Kris Haggblom

All rights reserved.

No part of this book may be used or reproduced in any manner whatsoever without written permission except in the case of brief quotations embodied in critical articles and reviews. Members of educational institutions and organizations wishing to photocopy any of the work for classroom use, or authors, artists and publishers who would like to obtain permission for any material in the work, should contact the publisher.

Published by Poetic Justice Books
Port Saint Lucie, Florida
www.poeticjusticebooks.com

ISBN: 978-1-950433-22-3

10 9 8 7 6 5 4 3

contents

The Panther and the Mermaid 3
Deserted 5
Bandages 6
Class Distinction 8
Spayed 10
It 12
On Leaving the Love Nest 14
Inter-Disciplinary 15
All's Fair 16
Praying for Nostalgia to Set In 18
Papercut 20
Tines 21
Crutchprints 22
Harlem 23
Mishawaka Wetlands 24
Conviction 26

Princes
&
Tides

THE PANTHER AND THE MERMAID

There she sat down
In her seaweed crown
On a rock by the side
Of the sea shore tide

She was free of human bothers
Such as taxes and strict fathers
The one thing the same with her life in the ocea
Was that she could feel every human emotion

She was all that a sailor could ever wish
Crystal-Eyed, witty and very smart
But even in the schools of fish
They don't teach how to mend a broken heart

One summer day in burning heat
The panther went stalking on padded feet
Thinking his maturing black velvet sins
As he suddenly spots her innocent fins

He attacked with his charm
Giving no time for alarm
Not long after their romance did commence
Passion had overpowered common sense

For many moons they secretly met
He gave perfection she wouldn't regret
She was too weak to play hard-to-get
Even when it was over she could never forget

Dawn Taggblom

He left with the force of an undertow
And not even the seagulls know
Why agony pierced her soul like hell
And her life seemed like an empty shell

He felt no mercy – he was proud and strong
Though he had memories of her hair so long
The very same sweet dreams that he did keep
Lived over and over in her aqua sleep

Animals always use what they learn
And one day he knew he would return
But meanwhile the waves themselves did moan
For the mermaid majestically waiting alone.

DESERTED

My soul is beached
Breathing in short, heavy gasps
For air that isn't there.

The sand is bleached
But covered with ugly tar
And littered with plastic containers.

I drift, the sand sifts
Beneath the fibres of me, pulsating in pain
Exhausted with the effort of every inch.

Like tinkerbell with Peter Pan,
I am faint, imploring the world to clap its hands
    For you, to stop Captain Jack Daniels
From killing you.

I can't do it alone. And no one applauds for us.

A transparent crab stares,
Indifferent to human snares.

Just think: if we didn't have souls
Our hearts would have no holes
For creatures to hide in.

BANDAGES

Self-hatred must be violet
Like the inside of my eyelids,
Because it is then
    That we can't turn away.

It must also be violent
Like the sound of chairs smashing
    Against the wall
TV antennas snapping
Bones breaking
Bruises purpling.

We cannot put our arms around ourselves
But we can self-destruct.

We crawl from paper to crystal
Yet we want more.

We are handed hours to daydream by the sea
Yet we can't bear to be alone
    With the surf washing distractions away.

We can reach out and stroke someone else's soul,
We can hug them and taste the hope –
But our hands recoil from the miserable mirror
And our jaws lock
    Our teeth clench
    In bitter decay.

We whine about broken hearts
While others go hungry
    Cannot even see the love on another's face to forget
    Cannot even hear a soft voice to miss
    Cannot even walk in a park to fall to their knees and cry.

Perhaps we can forgive ourselves
By crying enough for everyone else.

CLASS DISTINCTION

My pain is private
Hot tears on a puppy
Who hides nothing in her eyes

I can take my pain with me wherever I go
    (it is portable pain)
I can dine in on it
    Or take it out
I can even put it in the microwave
    To reheat later
    When I'm home alone
Or swirl it around and drink it down

Have I introduced you to my pain?
If you get to know it you will love it too.
It is exceptional, with its very own
    Plaques on the wall
Like exquisite perfume, unique to
    Every woman's pulses
A present from every man
    (Don't say he never gave you anything)

My pain is also the simmering scent of
    Pine needles on a summer day
A happy family in the yard, Mom's
    Dinner cooking away

It is the wail of a saxophone
The curve of a smile
There! It glows on the end of a cigarette.
Don't forget to put out my pain
    Before it starts a fire ...

SPAYED

It was between the two of them
The doctor
And her
(Patience).

He had to slice her
As he had been taught to do.
But her owners liked to think
He was a good doctor,
    A gentle doctor.

He had done her a favor
(not to mention the world)
To prevent the creation
Of more precious puppies –
The love so boundless
    And playful and free
Only to be killed in the road
Or starved to death.

He had to steel himself
    Against the fear and the trust
    Brimming in her eyes.
This part of her simply had to be removed.
He was a good doctor,
    A gentle doctor.

He sent her home where her family
    Lay and stroked her in silence.
They kept her warm, caressing away
    The pain and confusion.
They prayed for the life they once knew
    To return, only more
    Domesticated.

(It was not the doctor's fault.)

IT

Perhaps it was in the jersey owls
Who I first noticed at night
Alone, cold, exhilarated
In my grandmother's house.

I know it was there when
I'd hike through the woods
    The next morning,
Feeling the twigs snap
And sometimes running blind.

It was there in my grandfather's grip
As he sipped whiskey straight
    From the bottle he rocked on one knee
    With me, three, on the other.

It is in my father's eyes.
It is always in the tide
And herbal tea in me.

It is there when strangers mate,
Having picked up its scent
    On one another
Having recognized a gesture
    Of desperation.

I miss my mother's soothing hands
Smoothing my back,
Swallowing her own suffering
Telling me in silence all was okay
And almost sending it away.

It is hovering between friends,
A knowing nod ...
It lives among cicadas
In a sultry Florida swamp.

Again, you hear it in loud music
From a car on the Interstate.
It thrives in teenage jeans.

It makes us shudder
Yet we must embrace it
To survive.

ON LEAVING THE LOVE NEST

All furniture gone,
Shoulders back, I vacuumed on,
Suddenly hitting a hardened spot –
A six-month old, carpeted knot.

I crouched, creaking at midnight
At the absolute end of my lease;
I touched, gasping in grief
At the faint scent of sea spray.

Candle wax, carelessly left
On our first night of loving here –
An aqua torch on the cardboard side
Of a six-pack of our beer.

Like then, there now was nothing else
But passion in this place;
Yet all my scraping effort
    (my furious fingers bled)
This ecstasy would not erase.

INTER-DISCIPLINARY

Sometimes I wish you wouldn't
    Clear your throat in my head
Or cough, or laugh that love-of-life way,
Or push back your chair decidedly
Rolling over to conquer the computer's tasks ...
There's not enough room in head for you
    Sometimes –
Not for you to play with my cat,
Look woefully in my fridge,
Shift gears with a fabulous fist –
No room for any of that!
I'm sorry, but insurance forms,
Checkbooks all off balance,
Manuals to memorize,
And boxes to unpack
    Are in the way of you
    In my head today --
Not to mention I must think of you
    As dead today.

ALL'S FAIR

On the eve before the new war
My tea grows tasteless.
In one hour my nineteen-year-old cousin
Would have blood on the runway awaiting him,
His bride tucked safely in Mississippi,
His brother, in college, a new-age hippie.

In one hour the world would change again,
Shake up the sand and watch it sift
    Through glass upside-down,
Down there where triple A has no maps.
Eleven o'clock and all's fair. Those who know
where their children are, are crying.

I think of the haircut I hope to get tomorrow.
I think of invisible molecular death,
The labored sound of a surgeon's breath,
And the movie scenes I'd seen.
My grandpa, whom we never knew.
I hope it was quick and quiet.

On the eve before the new war
I feel the place on my breastbone
Where your hand pushed firmly against my heart
    Saying no let's not make it worse,
My mouth open in vain,
Two protests standing in a windstorm,
A Desert Shield.

I remain a prisoner of your war, though a
volunteer ... a casualty of your love.
At 11:15 I think to myself if I could guarantee
    The chance to free
Your wife and children forever, I might go too.
I am their unknown hero.

The soldiers will be yelling, I suppose
And rushing over dunes of youth,
Headlong harbingers of truth.
I imagine you'll protect the pretty eyes
In front of your TV, turning it off and
    Saying no let's not make it worse.
Me, I'd rather keep a hand on my breastbone
Alone with a lavender heart.

PRAYING FOR NOSTALGIA TO SET IN

I hold still,
Praying for nostalgia to set in,
Waiting for the wound to close,
Hoping the line of poison will not reach my heart.

My hatred bounces boundlessly
Off the black-green of your computer screen,
The hem of your running shorts
And the T-shirt you so easily replaced.

It ricochets from the shafts of hair
As you shake your gorgeous head
In conversations avoiding my name.

I hold still,
Wishing I didn't want you dead.

I bow my head,
Picturing a time when I can
Nod knowingly at the mention of you,
Not being overcome with chills,
The hair on my neck bristling,
Cringing from that stomach-punch,
That heated rush of lethal lust,
That demon-screaming denial of love done.

Mindful of the cost, I cannot move
To walk or drive to where you are,
Call long-distance, test resistance,
Torture my brain already beaten beyond recognition.

I hold still.

PAPERCUT

In just one of your lives,
We were but a small, quick mistake.

The psychic leaned forward,
Her long, graceful hands consoling:
The card bore a heart with three swords.

She said you would be my last test.

And so I stood,
Like Christ in Gethsemane, as you
    (unintentional devil)
Smiled across the grass,
Painting visions of warmth in your arms.

It took the strength of God
For me to break the silence
Of you holding a finger to your lips,
    Beckoning,
Stealing my breath like a cat from a baby.

TINES

Inadvertently touching your fork with mine,
I think of diners past in passion
Where you gladly shared my germs.

Our laughter silver,
Clinking warm ceramic souls.

Prongs pierce my silent palms,
Wincing at your small talk,
Bleeding sugar.

You say you cared for me –
Syllables spilling into your coffee,
Sweet and low.

Sipping tea, I muse how
You'd deny those three other words
From three other occasions.

I pretend you look older
Like I wouldn't lick your lips,
Feed you life, when you go blind.

I move my fork, hide a jitter,
Smile bitter, but it's ok;
We'd finished eating.

{February 14}

CRUTCHPRINTS

There they were, on the carpet
(or wall-to-wall rug)
Of my apartment building.

Press, poof.
Press, poof.

I am always so gentle
With myself (and my victims)
When it is all over.

We both wanted space
But I wanted you to fill mine
And me yours.
How sad (and scary)
There are spaces
We can never share.

When my mother was 29 I was 10,
Already confused by the stirrings of lust
In my little life.
It was not until she was 35
And nearly died
That I saw where her crutchprints went.

HARLEM

On a subway full of fearless faces
I began to forget you.

Token teeth gleaming beneath your dark
Satin head of Village hair,
Trump-Towering chest
Bumbling down Broadway
Public Library exhibits
In your expanded brain
For all to visit.

Not for ME, nor any of these souls
Bundled in stoic clusters
Or one blanket against old brick,
Sirens every 30 seconds,
A cathedral where I saw the Stones in spraypaint
Someone else with my ticket in the front row
Of that concert with you.

No, I'd rather smell the charcoal air,
Feeling radiator steam
Near people with no family dream
And no curtains.
123rd street is my stop –
This is where I GET OFF.

MISHAWAKA WETLANDS

Flying north from summer steam
To lands unseen, an Irish dream.
Bird lands with bruised wing, Yet restless.

Near the sacred banks of Lake Mary,
The Basilica preys silently
On all her deepest doubt,
Immaculate stains.

Just then, forced to be virgin again,
Sifting gold from greed,
Holy from hypocrisy.

The saints flanked by fireflies
and red brick
Where Reverend Hesburgh blessed the books
In glorious glass display.

Beneath the evergreens
Her beak begins to Bend, South.
Bless him! Curse him!
Let his beer and cigarettes be blasphemous.

Wishing, hearing hymns
Echo through ancient archways.

They could not mate here despite a fated
Soon-faded full moon.
No place for a great blue-jean heron
    To stand on one leg –
She trembled denial of earthly desire.

Does Faith wait for those beaten by land or by sea?
Alone with the Dome,
She'd found a safe home
For fervency.

CONVICTION

Like an eagle you stand flexed and poised
Atop the highest honor,
Offering Justice its finest hour,
The winds of Faith sometimes
Slowing to bare breezes
Through your feathers.

Those wings, though, that mighty chest!
No, the world has not yet seen your best –
No woman on Earth could ever find
A warmer heart or sharper mind.

In my prayers and in my tears
All birds sing to soothe away
The suffering of your years ...
Patience and Love can bring their own Reward;
Just keep your glance not Back
But Toward.

{my last poem}

Princes & Tides

Princes & Tides is a collection of poetry spanning twenty years. The earliest poem was composed in 1977 and the final piece in 1996. Dawn Taggblom has vowed to not write another poem until certain miscarriages of justice have been rectified.

Princes & Tides was originally published as a limited edition chapbook by SpiNDec Press in 2018.

www.ingramcontent.com/pod-product-compliance
Lightning Source LLC
Chambersburg PA
CBHW030104100526
44591CB00008B/274